time
to leave

marina aimée

ISBN: 9798337767833

time to leave is the third *mini* book of the series *LITTLE DROPS COLLECTION*, a total of 12 books that will be released once per month during a year (August 2024-August 2025). Marina Aimée is the author of all these *mini* books. Find more information about the project on my Instagram account (@marinaaimeepoetry) and find the rest of the books on Amazon.

Marina Aimée self-published her first poetry book in English, *how to survive yourself*, in 2022. In 2023, she published a second one: *patterns to destroy*. She is currently releasing *LITTLE DROPS COLLECTION*.

The poet lives full time traveling and finds joy and happiness in the people she meets along the way, the cultures she learns about and the countries she gets to visit every year. She is immersed in an endless journey of self-love.

She once felt a huge hatred towards herself but learned how to destroy all the harmful patterns and change them for kind words, affection and art.

You can purchase her books in English on Amazon and find her poetry on Instagram: @marinaaimeepoetry

time
to leave

i loved you with my whole heart
but i needed myself back

time to leave

i still cry
when i remember
what we could have been
if we had tried harder

you were scared of feeling
and i wanted to feel it all

you asked me
why i had to write
twelve books
to get over you

love,

i needed to write
twelve books just
to understand
we couldn't be together

getting over you
that doesn't take
a bunch of poetry books
that's gonna take my whole life

when you ask for the truth
you also have to be ready
to listen to one that you don't like

only you can save yourself
because no one else can do it
the way you need it to be done

you made me see
love is not always *easy*
but it is supposed to be
light
and warm
and soft

time to leave

you planted seeds in my garden
so all my favorite flowers
could grow there

i'm looking for you
everywhere
but i just find you
in the darkest places
of my memory

my life is full of love
since the day i met you

marina aimée

once your purpose
touches your soul
it will never leave

hey
i just wanted to tell you
how grateful i am for having you in my life

i know i can learn from this
but i can't help feeling that
i lost all these years of my life
and i'll never get them back

i'm too busy working on myself
to focus my energy on people
who aren't even sure if they love me

marina aimée

if i break
will someone pick up the pieces
and help me put them together?

i was definitely born
in this body
in this family
in these circumstances
so i could heal
in this lifetime
the sorrow my soul
was carrying all along

knowing the truth
is extremely painful
but also liberating

please love me today
just in case tomorrow
i'm not here anymore

do they know that even if i'm not
the person they expected me to be
i'm the happiest version of myself?

loving you
is like feeling the wind
through the window
of a bus speeding
on a dangerous cliff
it's scary
but also an adictive
rush of adrenaline

i'm relearning
how to love myself
and the first step
is accepting i made
the terrible mistake
of ceasing to be mine
so i could be yours

when was the last time you were happy
and you knew it at that exact moment?

do you let people into
your life who will hurt you
because
a part of yourself still
feels you don't deserve
to be treated better?

i'm sometimes a window
through which people
can see other possibilities

i'm sometimes a mirror
through which people
can see themselves

the real blessing is when
solitude doesn't feel like
loneliness anymore

maybe you feel
like you're about to fall
because you're holding on
to something
that isn't there anymore

i crave
the day i trust people again
the day i can put my heart
in someone's hands
without the inmense fear
that they will break it

sometimes
you want with your whole heart
to stay in a place where there's
no longer room for you
and the more you fight to fit
the more that's gonna hurt you

maybe the right answer
was to ignore the heart
and for once
just for once
listen to my head

i still miss you
but at least i understood
i never needed you

will the heaviness
on my chest
disappear
if i let you go?

marina aimée

i still burst into tears
in the middle of the street
when someone says my name
in the exact same way you used to

time to leave

this chapter of my life it's called
i'm not settling for less than i deserve

marina aimée

i don't love you
i love the person
i thought you were
but being aware of it
doesn't change the fact
that the love is still there

the people i love the most
are always the fastest to run away

when my head screams a bit louder
is when i need the silence outside

is there something wrong with me
and that's the reason why love
never works out for me?

sometimes
i need so little
to stay in places
where i know
i will be hurt

please
next time
i tell you
i'm fine
don't believe it

when i opened
the door
of my heart
to your love
and you called it
home
i didn't expect
your love
to stay there
even long after
you had left

i don't know who you are anymore
but you're still so alive inside of me

you sleep next to someone else
and i'm sleeping next to the memory of you

now that i know
i won't see you again
i choose to remember
your laugh filling with joy my heart
instead of your eyes full of rage

flowers in my hair
hope in my heart
spring has arrived

it hurts so much to let you go
because you loved me in a way
that i hadn't learned to love myself yet

maybe you would like
to remember
good girls
also know how to fight

time to leave

i'll braid flowers in my hair
so the bees know where to go
when winter arrives and the garden
is cold
empty
dead
the grave of the time when you loved me
i'll braid flowers in my hair
because i'm spring
color
life
the reborn of the ghost you left behind

today
dance
as if you were never
gonna listen to music again

rise your soul high
and trust the universe
will take care of you

rise your dreams high
and trust the universe
will be listening to you

marina aimée

i just understood
i can be happy without you
so you have no more power over me

i loved myself
with the same fury
everyone else hated me
and that's how i learned to bloom

Printed in Great Britain
by Amazon

49567330R00034